YOU
DESERVE
BETTER

ABOUT THE BOOK

How can I work so that my clients receive daily attention that results in the best possible chance of securing their long-term needs and goals? How do I ensure I am the financial advisor people refer to as "accessible"? And how do I put the advise back in advising?

These are just a few of the questions Todd VanDenburg posed to himself when he first started out over a decade ago in the financial services industry. Based on his own personal experience as an investor who, like many others, experienced some potentially unnecessary losses during the dot.com bubble, Todd decided not only to thoroughly study and learn the business of financial services, but to build his business by applying the same standards he would for his mother—were she sitting across the desk from him—for all of his clients.

You Deserve Better provides an enlightening look at the type of relationship and level of service we all can and should expect from our financial advisor. The book shows that while becoming accustomed to feeling like a number may be acceptable in some facets of our modern-day lives, the one-size-fits-all policy does not fit when it comes to how we manage our money and plan our retirement. If ever there was a place and a time for individualized attention, it is in our financial advisor's office and it is now—particularly after having seen just how vulnerable our nest eggs can become due to situations completely out of our control. Some of the old adages regarding financial planning no longer hold true, and the experts and analysts will talk until their hair turns blue. *You Deserve Better* takes an energetic and emphatic look at just how valuable a financial advisor who is truly invested in your lifelong goals can be.

ABOUT THE AUTHOR

A self-proclaimed lifelong learner, Todd VanDenburg began pushing himself, and pushing the envelope, first in his elementary school math and science classes, in college, and also as a young man in the military. Moving up through the chain of command early, and then deciding to embark on a career in software and systems analysis, Todd found work that engaged him: looking at large complex problems, and solving them in the most effective and efficient way possible. When he decided to then switch lanes and become a financial advisor, his desire and flare for the human relations side of problem-solving fully flourished— and he has never looked back.

Advising with a heart—and a whole lot of mental muscle, Todd is well known in his field as an innovator who truly puts his clients' needs and goals first. A former Valley of the Moon Rotary Club member and Paul Harris Fellow, Todd continues to support his local community through a variety of donations and sponsorships.

Remaining accessible as his business continues to grow, and educating clients in the most respectful and professional manner possible, Todd has created a family business that truly has, over the years, been run with his family alongside him. His wife, an avid reader, and his twin daughters (one attends Loyola Marymount and the other University of San Diego), have all reaped the benefits of working in a relationship-focused environment. VanDenburg Capital Management thrives because its clients thrive; Todd VanDenburg's passion is his clients' wellbeing.

YOU DESERVE BETTER

WHAT YOU SHOULD
REALLY EXPECT
FROM YOUR
FINANCIAL ADVISOR

TODD VANDENBURG

VanDenburg Capital Management

To my Mother...

*For providing me with the
best foundation that anyone
could ever want or need.*

To my Wife...

*For supporting my entrepreneurial spirit
and for partnering with me
to build on that foundation
to become the man that I am today.*

CONTENTS

Chapter 1

Are You Getting What You Deserve?

"Be a yardstick of quality. Some people aren't used to an environment where excellence is expected."
—Steve Jobs

"I can't believe that you're calling me back so quickly, Todd. You do know that it's seven thirty p.m., right? You should be with your family!"

It's true—a client called my office after business hours and I returned the call that night. Not every call requires this kind of attention, but my policy is that when a client calls with a serious concern, I try to answer them before they go to sleep that night. The research is clear enough—stress can reduce our lifespan. We all know too that money is one of the greatest causes of stress—so why would I allow any of my clients' questions about their money to go unanswered overnight?

This is just one example of my personal commitment to providing superior service ("Four Seasons" service, if you will) to all of my clients. This laser-like focus on the needs of my clients is exemplified by

THREE GUIDING PRINCIPLES that my employees and I follow every day. They are:

1. What am I doing to help my clients today?

2. What am I doing to improve the business so that I can provide my clients with better service today?

3. What am I doing to improve myself so that I add more value to the business and can do a better job for my clients today?

As you can see, each of these guiding principles begins and ends with a single goal: to do something every day that is, ultimately, of direct benefit to my clients. Many days, what this looks like in practice might be something as fundamental as communication—returning client calls promptly, or maybe reaching out via phone, letter, or e-mail, simply to catch up, to discuss any potentially concerning major US economic news, or to check in if I sense something isn't right closer to home.

Other days, I might call on my twenty-year background in software development to create and leverage technology that helps me monitor my clients' accounts in ways that almost no other advisor can. I've designed custom software that I run against all the activity on my clients' accounts to identify potential areas of interest or concern. I know the first time they use their debit card, and I'm aware when they write a check for an amount that is greater than normal. With this level of monitoring and service, I can call up my client and say, "Hey! I see you used your debit card for the first time. You've never used it before," or "I've never known you to write a check for over $5,000. Is everything okay? Was that you?"

Said another way, I look at everything I do through the prism of what I would want if I were on the other side of the desk.

I also think of the things the typical financial advisor does:

✓ **Is my client using their money wisely and enjoying it fully?**

✓ **Will it last as long as they live?**

✓ **If they have more than they are ever going to spend, are we doing enough for their heirs?**

But unlike many financial advisors, I am also thinking beyond my clients getting what they deserve financially—I aim to give them what they deserve emotionally, too.

Far too many times, I've heard of situations where an investor says, "I didn't call my advisor because I know he's really busy with his other clients." There is danger in that. You have an advisor precisely because you want to make decisions with someone educated at your side. I am at your side. You deserve to have an advisor who treats your financial picture—and its inherent emotional components—with respect. The first step toward discovering and building a long-lasting professional relationship with your financial advisor is understanding what you deserve. There are certain standards you have a right to hold your advisor to, and the right advisor will gladly discuss and uphold these standards.

> *The first step toward discovering and building a long-lasting professional relationship with your financial advisor is understanding what you deserve.*

It's true, we all have busy lives to lead, and sometimes it's convenient to comfort ourselves with the old adage "No news is good news." If we aren't hearing from our lawyer or our tax specialist or our financial advisor, we assume we are in good hands. We also often make certain assumptions about the kinds of things that our trusted professionals are doing for us when we're not with them, but are our expectations in line with what typically happens?

5 EXPECTATIONS

EXPECTATION #1
Advisors spend the majority of their time managing investments.

The reality is that up until very recently, the vast majority of financial advisors made their living from commissions, which often meant they needed to spend the majority of their time on the acquisition of new clients and the generation of investment transactions. It can be to your advantage to have an advisor who works on a fee basis, and is therefore more focused on managing your assets than on transactions that generate commissions. Because a fee-based advisor is compensated according to the amount of assets under management, his income is based on how well he manages your money—talk about a built-in incentive to create a win-win situation! A fee-based system can also remove potential conflicts of interest, keeping the focus on you and not on any given product.

As a fee-based advisor, I sustain my business and provide for my family not based on the transactions of the day, but by paying attention to my clients' portfolios and financial goals. My calendar is not filled with appointments to sign up new clients every day. To the contrary, my calendar is filled up with whatever my clients need me to attend to. In a nutshell, a fee-based advisor like me doesn't get paid big commissions up front. Instead, we have to earn the right to help you work toward your goals every single day.

EXPECTATION #2
Advisors will treat me like an individual, not like a number.

Over the years, advisors have developed many models to use as a basis for managing their clients' assets—*all* their clients' assets. This means that too often all clients with a given investment objective or risk tolerance end up being asked to sell everything they own so they can purchase shares of x, y, and z (so that they are invested according to the advisor's "model"), regardless of what they already own or want.

VanDenburg Capital Management does not subscribe to this one-size-fits-all mentality. We believe you deserve to be treated in a way that is unique to you and to your specific situation and needs. For example, if you've owned a stock for decades, chances are there could be a pretty hefty tax bill if you sell. In this case, does it really make sense to sell just so you can buy other investments that fit into a specific, precut model?

Similarly, if a stock has just recently come onto your radar and you would like to invest in it, why should you be prevented from doing so? When it comes to your money and your livelihood, recognize your right to a financial management experience that is tailored to your specific needs and goals.

Being treated as an individual goes beyond your portfolio—your advisor needs to understand your lifestyle, your needs, and your dreams. Just as people often prefer local banks because the tellers know who they are, who their kids are, and what their lives are like, many people seek out advisors who can offer that personal touch. The individualized attention you will receive at VanDenburg Capital Management may at first come as somewhat of a shock, because we treat you with a small-town familiarity backed by extensive financial knowledge.

EXPECTATION #3
Advisors will adapt their investment strategies to a changing environment.

For decades now, politicians and financial analysts have been fond of the slogan "A rising tide lifts all boats," but the other side of that coin—as our nation experienced in 2008—is Warren Buffett's truism, "Only when the tide goes out do you discover who's been swimming naked." The belief that a rising tide will lift all boats has given rise to many different investment strategies, but there is one that we often find problematic for retirees: the concept of buy and hold.

Sitting on a given investment has its advantages—sometimes—but when it doesn't, **your advisor needs not only to alert you to the appropriate time to get out**, but to make sure that you actually do it. In other words, it might make perfect sense to stand in the same place (that is, to hold the same investments) for a long time, but when you feel the ground start to vibrate under your feet and you hear the whistle of the oncoming train, you deserve to have someone pull you off the tracks before the train comes!

> *Sitting on a given investment has its advantages—sometimes—but when it doesn't, your advisor needs not only to alert you to the appropriate time to get out, but to make sure that you actually do it.*

Another common rule of thumb is subtracting your age from one hundred to find out what percentage of your money you should invest in stocks vs. bonds—meaning, as you age you should increase your allocation in bonds and reduce your exposure to stocks. This approach may have worked in the past, but with interest rates at near all-time lows (and accordingly, bond values near all-time highs), is today the right time to be increasing your exposure to bonds? We know that as interest rates start to rise, bond values often go down, so if you think interest rates are going to rise, is it really a good time to be making this transition (no matter what the adage might tell you to do)?

All this is to say that **just because something worked ten years ago, or worked in your portfolio in the past, that does not mean it will in the future.** Said another way, if you wanted to drive your car somewhere, would you make all of your decisions about what to do next based upon what you see in your rearview mirror (an approach that we don't recommend anyone try out)? You need an advisor who is up-to-date on what's happening in the market and is not afraid to let go of what worked in the past but may no longer be viable.

EXPECTATION #4
Advisors are accessible.

People want to know that they can reach their advisor. You might have a question or a concern, or you might need to set up a meeting—and you should be able to get in touch with your advisor in a timely fashion. Again, advisors who are paid on commission often need to fill their calendars with new clients because they have to generate transactions in order to put food on the table. Sadly, this often leaves very little time to meet with existing clients.

To be clear, I am not this type of advisor! Not only am I fee-based, but when I call my clients, it is to see what I can do for them, not the other way around. In addition, when my clients call me, I do my level best to be available either to take the call immediately or to get back to them within a few hours (at most). When a client calls asking to get together to discuss some important financial issues, I often meet with them the same day if that is what they want (or need).

Unfortunately, I hear from people who have left their advisor to work with us that trying to get an appointment with their old advisor was like trying to get an appointment with a highly specialized physician—they put you on the calendar for a month or more out. We, on the other hand, believe that meeting the client at *their* earliest convenience is the kind of service everybody deserves, and it is certainly the kind of service we strive to deliver daily.

EXPECTATION #5
Advisors will keep me from making financial mistakes.

The primary rule of working with people is that the customer is always right, but sometimes this can mean your advisor might allow you to make a poor investment choice in order to keep you happy. Trust me, you do not want this kind of advisor.

The person whom you have entrusted with the important job of managing your money must truly *advise* you, in the strictest sense of the word. You've done your job and earned and saved your money; your advisor's job, as a professional educated in the field of investments, is to help you keep and manage it. Or, if you will, to get your money to work as hard for you as you worked to earn it.

Fiduciaries aside, most advisors are under no real obligation to prevent you from making a mistake. If you are interested in buying gold, a commission-based broker might provide a gold mutual fund and outline the risks, but they might not go beyond that. They might not ask further critical questions, such as, "Do I think that this is a good investment? Is it the proper amount? Is my client overallocated? Should my client be invested in something else?"

In order for you to get your money's worth, your advisor needs to be able ask himself those questions, present them to you if necessary, and then be ready to take action. It's certainly fair—and often standard practice—for an advisor to tell you the potential consequences of your actions, but you should be able to depend on him to go the extra mile each and every time, to keep you from making overly emotional or potentially underinformed decisions.

> *It's certainly fair—and often standard practice—for an advisor to tell you the potential consequences of your actions, but you should be able to depend on him to go the extra mile each and every time, to keep you from making overly emotional or potentially underinformed decisions.*

Many people also think their financial advisors function the same way doctors do: "Above all else, do no harm." Unfortunately, that standard isn't typically how the industry works—but it's what you deserve when you go to someone for help.

By following my guiding principles and exceeding my clients' expectations, I have built a business on a solid foundation of mutual respect, shared success, and satisfactory long-term relationships. Providing insight into each client's unique situation builds trust, and with that trust established, I can focus all my energies on managing my clients' investments, regardless of their net worth or how long they've been with me.

As you read on, I invite you to consider the expectations I have outlined above. Review too the principles that all employees of VanDenburg Capital Management practice on a daily basis. Ask yourself what is important to you in a professional relationship in general, and what you expect of your financial advisor in particular. What are your standards, and does your financial advisor meet them— or better yet, exceed them?

CHAPTER 2

My Story: Sergeant by Day, College Student by Night

"We do more before 9:00 a.m. than most people do all day."
—1981 Army TV commercial

Throughout my entire life, my mother has been my greatest source of inspiration. I am the thoughtful, hardworking, and successful man I am now because her unflinching belief in working hard and doing your best was passed on to me in my youth. My mother wasn't much of a believer in luck, and neither am I; what others call luck, I was taught to see as preparation meeting opportunity. That major-league player hits a home run not because of luck, but because his twenty years in a batting cage have trained him to do what he has to do when the perfect pitch is thrown.

Growing up, I watched my mother do everything she had to do to put food on the table and to make sure that for all of the sports I played—and I played many—I had the right gear. Despite having to hold down two jobs, my mom made it to every game that she could. Childhood friends whom I keep in touch with today still recall my mother in the bleachers; they all say, "Who could forget her enthusiasm?" My mother was not a hair over five feet tall, but she always gave 100 percent, and so do I.

Studying for an associate's degree in computer science, I learned many acronyms, but there is one that I have embraced since the first day I heard it: DADIE. DADIE stands for Define, Analyze, Design, Implement, and Evaluate. Have a problem that needs to be solved? Apply this process and check your results—if you don't achieve the results you are wishing for, run the process again.

I graduated from high school at the end of my junior year, and because the cost of a college education was out of reach, I decided to join the military. My father and grandfather had been in the service, so it was the natural thing to do. When the Air Force recruiter I was set to meet with didn't show up for our appointment, I met instead with an Army recruiter. I sat and chatted with him for some time, took a test, and was told my score was so high I could choose any job in the military I wanted. The Air Force guy hadn't shown, but the Army recruiter showed me how I could still get into an airplane, even though I was only seventeen and a half. I chose to work in aerial surveillance and reconnaissance, flying as the "right-seater" in an OV-1 Mohawk.

In the military, I built on the fundamentals my mother had instilled in me: to work hard and give it my best. The military laid out a set of policies and procedures—a way of organizing and planning—that I grasped immediately. In aerial surveillance and reconnaissance, back in those days before everything was done by drones, we had to plan our missions—what our course would be, how we would fly in to avoid detection, what equipment we would use, and how we would remain exposed for the least amount of time before exiting the area.

The methodical and sequential nature of everything we had to do to accomplish a mission and stay alive appealed to me (the US wasn't at war with anyone when I served, but we had to plan as if we were). Work hard, give it your best, use your smarts and build on them, and stay organized—at a very young age, I was learning a recipe for success.

At the same time I was serving on active duty, I was attending night school at a junior college near the base, in Fort Hood, Texas. Studying for an associate's degree in computer science, I learned many acronyms, but there is one that I have embraced since the first day I heard it: DADIE. **DADIE** stands for **Define, Analyze, Design, Implement,** and **Evaluate.** Have a problem that needs to be solved? Apply this process and check your results—if you don't achieve the results you are wishing for, run the process again.

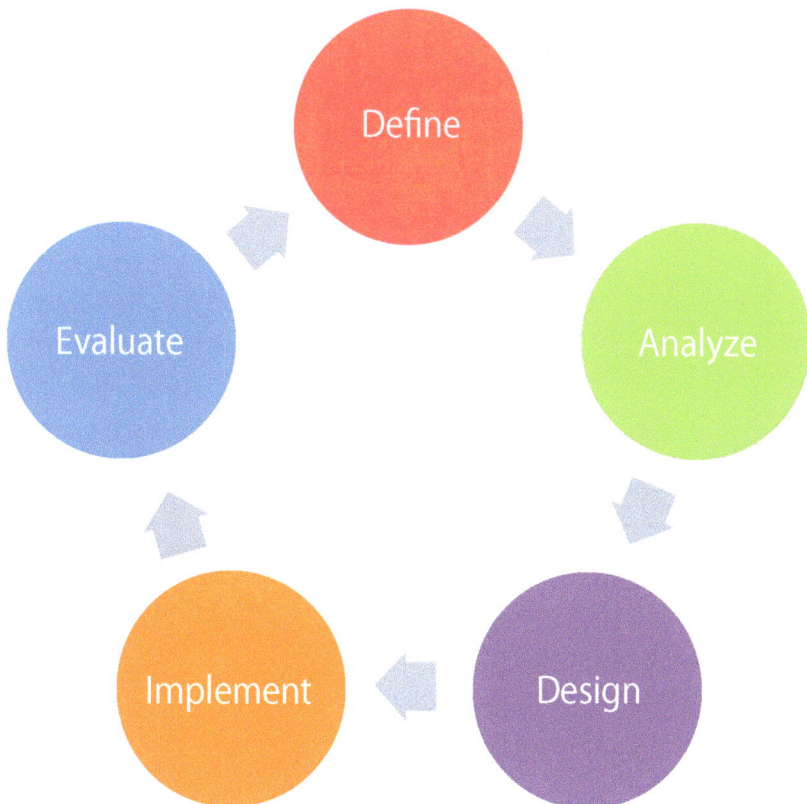

As a teenager, I chose to become part of a very exclusive team—from 1981 to 1983 there were roughly eighty-five aerial surveillance and reconnaissance guys in the US Army. And though the practical applications of such a specialized job might have been few in the outside world, those three years were hardly a waste of time. Before I had even turned twenty, I had learned not only to head into any project with a plan, but to use DADIE to work through that plan. I stuffed my head in those years with computer languages and I fueled my internal drive to not just "be all that I could be," as the old Army advertisements went, but to be and do much, much more.

> *As a financial advisor, I am working on behalf of my clients by six thirty or seven a.m. daily. When the stock market opens, I'm on it. By nine a.m., when most people are just unlocking their office doors, I have already done most of the analysis I need to do on any trades and rebalancing.*

As a financial advisor, I am working on behalf of my clients by six thirty or seven a.m. daily. **When the stock market opens, I'm on it.** By nine a.m., when most people are just unlocking their office doors, I have already done most of the analysis I need to do on any trades and rebalancing. I can then focus 100 percent of my energies on taking care of my clients by performing due diligence on new and existing investments, watching market and economic conditions, and so on. Those who entrust me with their life savings have given me the highest honor, and I take that responsibility very seriously. That means I spend the vast majority of my time trying to do things that directly (or indirectly) benefit my clients; it means I never lose sight of the guiding principles I outlined in Chapter One.

My route to becoming a financial advisor, in hindsight, feels like a clearly cut trail that my mother initially set me on. In my first post-military position, I worked for CSAA (California State Automobile Association) as a claims adjuster. I was promoted as fast as anyone could be promoted, and when presented with an offer to attend a computer-programmer trainee class, I jumped. After a series of interviews and tests, eight people from across the company were offered the class, and I was one of them. After continuing on for several years with CSAA, I briefly returned to the Army (as part of the Army Reserves) and trained as a Korean linguist. It seemed clear to me that learning more about things outside the US might help me in the future, so as I have done so many times since, I added another tool to my tool belt—even though I wasn't exactly sure yet how I would use it.

Because I had been promoted in the minimum amount of time you can be promoted in the military, by the time I was training as a linguist I was already a sergeant. Here I was, twenty-five years old, and I was the class leader, responsible for many younger soldiers who were, in almost all cases, experiencing the military for the first time. My time in the military was exciting and wonderful, and I believe the military benefits young people by instilling in them usable and crucial skills, in addition to fundamental values such as responsibility and commitment. But at a certain point, I knew I would not make a good military careerist, because I had too much of an entrepreneurial spirit. The urge to work in a field that allowed me to apply DADIE to the bigger picture kept gnawing at me.

All my life, since the time I watched my mother as she did her bookkeeping job, I've had a head for numbers. When computers shifted from being accessible only to large companies (via the mainframe) to being accessible to almost everyone (via the PC), I kept pace. After my second tour in the military, I returned briefly to CSAA—which gladly welcomed me back—but after a while I could no longer resist the urge to take a leap out on my own. In line with the concept of maximizing my strengths and minimizing my weaknesses, I decided to leave my full-time job with CSAA and start my own software consulting firm, which I named Wise Computer Consultants, in honor of my wise wife's maiden name: Wise.

From the very beginning, I had a knack and the skills for understanding a person's or a company's problems. I could ask them to describe to me what they wanted and needed, and where needs or goals were not being met, and I often solved their problems in record time. In fact, many clients who had hired me to fulfill a ninety-day contract asked me to stay on for much longer—because I could often do what took most people ninety days in significantly less time.

My mother had taught me the basics—come to every engagement ready to work hard, work smart, and give it my all. The military added to that a deep knowledge and appreciation for structure and rigor. The clients I worked with over my roughly twenty years in technology told me they had never experienced anyone like me—I could apply DADIE to their specific objectives, give each project my laser-like focus, and help them succeed.

I consulted in industries as diverse as banking, insurance, and telecommunications, and although I approached my work from a problem-solving point of view, I also learned quite a lot about my clients' businesses. Yes, I created solutions and applied them, but I never simply slapped on a solution and walked away. By truly learning what each business did and how they did it, I learned where they needed help.

For example, when I worked for a Colorado-based start-up telecommunications company whose sales team was losing days at a time offering pricing solutions to potential clients, I discovered that most of these potential clients were just shopping around. Gathering a small team of people, I set about creating a solution I called *indicative pricing*, which allowed the sales team to offer a rough price for a product in minutes rather than in days. This solution enabled the sales team to spend more time on activity that had a higher probability of close (and that generated more revenue for the company).

Because my overall goal in consulting for any company or client has always been to find the best solution to a given problem, some of the solutions I have come up with have had more to do with bigger-picture processes than with specific technological conclusions. For example, when I first became a computer programmer with CSAA, I was assigned to better document all of the membership department's programs that were run on a periodic basis (daily, weekly, etc.), so that others could more easily understand the many components that made up the membership system.

After giving this assignment much thought (and again, back in the mid-'80s, computer technology was nothing like it is today), I decided that since a picture was worth a thousand words, I would create a system-flow diagram using an old green plastic IBM flow-charting template that looked something like a stencil. On one page, I described all of the computer programs that ran on a daily basis; on another page, all of the programs that ran on a weekly basis; on yet another page, those that ran on a monthly basis. Once completed, this diagram was used for many years, long after I was gone, to show others how everything worked.

This is one of many examples of how **the DADIE process that I learned in my first computer class in 1981 helped me apply a structured problem-solving methodology t**o almost every problem I have encountered over the past thirty-some years, whether it was in technology or in financial services.

Working in technology for almost two decades, I was able to educate myself about the ins and outs of a wide range of businesses. I learned to deeply understand an industry's challenges and struggles, and most important, I learned that no solution can ever be applied in isolation. I carry this knowledge with me as a financial advisor, and when a client comes to me and says, "Here's $50,000—let's see what you can do with it," I say, in short, that it really isn't in their best interest to put blinders on me like they would a horse drawing a carriage through Central Park. It is in their best interest to see what I can do with their $50,000 in relation to all of the other investments they have, and in relation to what their overall objective and risk tolerance is. Just as nobody should walk into a doctor's office and not alert the doctor to their entire medical history first, nobody should walk into their financial advisor's office and say, "Just do it."

> *...I am not the kind of financial advisor who will tell you to buy and hold and then kick my feet back.*

Also, I am not the kind of financial advisor who will tell you to buy and hold and then kick my feet back. As a fee-based advisor, my success depends entirely on how well I attend to and manage your finances. Many financial advisors are commission based, and as such are only held to what is often referred to as a suitability standard, meaning they only have to reasonably believe that any recommendations made are suitable for their clients in terms of the client's financial needs, objectives, and unique circumstances. On the other hand, I, as a fee-based fiduciary, don't just find you what is suitable, but what is *best* for you. Therefore, when making a recommendation, I look at the world of investments, as opposed to specific, potentially proprietary products, to find a solution that is both suitable and appropriate given all of your other investments, your given risk tolerance, and your investment objectives.

As you have probably guessed by now, sitting still has never been my thing—I am 100 percent my mother's son. When I was in the military, I was also in night school. When I returned to college in my late thirties to finish my bachelor's degree, I did so at night while holding down a full-time job during the day. When I worked for AFLAC and MetLife, I acquired some useful tools and got all the necessary licenses—and still I wanted more. Now, as the owner of my own business, I continue my education by taking a mix of technology and financial courses.

When I discovered that one could become a licensed professional fiduciary in California without needing to get any securities licenses, I registered for the courses—not because I planned to change careers, but because of what I discovered a licensed professional fiduciary might be able to provide my clients.

Seeing so many families torn apart after the death of a parent, I have always wondered if there were a better way to separate the grieving from the trustee experience. That is, if a family of three siblings had just lost their last parent, and the eldest child had been named trustee, how could that difficult role be eliminated—or changed? Suggesting to clients that they hire a professional fiduciary to act as their trustee is just one way I've found I can help them when it comes to the bigger picture—the one that includes reducing as much stress as possible when challenging financial and emotional times arise.

I am a lifelong learner so that I can provide the best service for my clients. If I'm not trying to improve myself, I just don't feel right—and this philosophy applies to my personal as well as my professional life. My wife has worked alongside me for years as a partner in the office as well as on the home front. Together we have faced and surmounted many of the same challenges most families face—such as getting our twin daughters ready for college. My wife has never wavered when faced with the unique challenges of working together as a couple to make a family business succeed.

Our daughters have also worked in our office, and it is because of this close-knit, all-for-one-and-one-for-all environment we have created that we find it so natural to extend ourselves in a similar way with our clients. The family business mindset that my wife and I have created is so strong that even though my wife has started to reduce the amount of time she spends at the office (stepping away for the first time in our long professional history together), and even though our daughters are fleeing the nest, our service to our clients will not change.

> *...while I am always trying to learn new things and find new ways to be of value, I am not doing so because I want to be a little bit of something for everyone. Instead, I'd prefer to be everything to a select few—meaning I will never place the growth of my practice above the high level of service and care I provide my clients.*

When we say we are a family business, we also mean we treat everyone who walks through our doors like family. My clients hire me to do an excellent job with their money, and being excellent is the reason I wake up in the morning. I do what I saw my mother do—and I hope my children and their children recognize just how far working hard and doing your best can take you. That said, **while I am always trying to learn new things and find new ways to be of value, I am not doing so because I want to be a little bit of something for everyone. Instead, I'd prefer to be everything to a select few—meaning I will never place the growth of my practice above the high level of service and care I provide my clients.**

CHAPTER 3

I'm Not a Genius, But I Do Try to Invest Like One

"We cannot solve our problems with the same thinking we used when we created them."
—Albert Einstein

Some kids have a knack for numbers. In the sixth grade, I liked math so much—and was so good at it—I was selected to attend a class at the local community college. Having a bona fide professor assign us the task of landing an imaginary lunar module on the moon—using numbers to calculate thrust, fuel usage, and the effects of gravity—was so much more thrilling than elementary school word problems involving the simple trading of apples and oranges among three friends.

Since I was drawn to numbers, you can imagine my excitement when I learned that different numbering systems existed. Binary numbers—I can't tell you what a concept that was to my young mind back in the mid-'70s! There were murmurings, too, of how binary numbers were being used in these newfangled machines called computers. Of course computers back then were monolith-sized mainframes that held about the same processing capacity as my cell phone does today, but from an early age I kept my ears open to the talk of how computers were going to revolutionize the world. Everything seemed to rely on numbers.

Fast-forward to not more than a decade later, and there I was, a young man in the Army, taking night courses at college and attending a technology seminar in Texas. A wiry, vibrant man took the stage and launched into a speech that hooked us all: America was going to become more efficient and productive than ever, thanks to computers. The workweek would be shortened and people would be able to share documents over long distances quickly without using stamps and post offices and mail carriers. Computers would change where people lived and worked—imagine! The US government was learning how to use smaller and faster computers, and this man was helping.

This man was Ross Perot, founder of EDS and future candidate for president of the United States, and of course he was dead right about the future of technology (with the possible exception of its impact on the length of the workweek). He was a man ahead of his time.

Ross Perot was one of the many smart guys I listened to. From the time I was a kid, I always wanted to listen to people who were smarter than me—I wanted to stay ahead of the curve. In one of those night classes I took as a young sergeant, I remember one instructor saying to the class, "Pretend I'm a computer. Tell me how to smoke a cigarette." There were no computers in classrooms at that time, but the task seemed easy enough. One classmate blurted out, "Open the pack." With that, the instructor proceeded to rip the pack in half with his bare hands, destroying all the cigarettes. *Aha!* I thought to myself. *We have to be specific.*

The pack-of-cigarettes lesson didn't spur me to become a computer guy then and there, but it did spark my interest. I decided that no matter what I chose to do in life, I would master technology. The concept of constructing programs at a fundamental, step-by-step level appealed to the way my mind worked. I enrolled in a variety of computer programming courses (Assembler, Fortran, COBOL, Visual Basic, HTML, etc.), and as noted in the first chapter, eventually took my first job out of the military with CSAA.

In the late '80s—again, always on the lookout for new ways of doing things faster, smarter, and better—I was introduced to Motorola's concept of "structured methodologies," specifically as it was used for software development. It was right up my alley in terms of how it outlined an approach to solving problems in a methodical, logical way. Motorola's

To this day, I seek out the smart guys. Specifically, when it comes to smarts in the financial services industry, I look for people who use math-based strategies and smart technology in order to navigate the world of investments.

concept eventually became known as **Six Sigma**. When Jack Welch later spoke of Six Sigma in terms of his "continuous improvement" philosophy, naturally, I paid attention.

To this day, I seek out the smart guys. Specifically, when it comes to smarts in the financial services industry, I look for people who use math-based strategies and smart technology in order to navigate the world of investments. The goal of a Six Sigma approach is to provide a service or manufacture a product with the fewest problems or failures. Six Sigma has a success rate of 99.99966 percent, meaning that for approximately every four million products a manufacturer might produce, only one should be a dud.

In the financial services industry, of course, it is impossible to promise such a high rate of success because markets fluctuate, investors define "success" in different ways, and a hundred factors are not under the direct control of financial advisors. However, in my business, I do pull from that Six Sigma concept—if I can't find a math-based reason for a given action, I probably shouldn't do it. I work from a philosophy

6σ

Six Sigma logo

that you can't fix what you can't measure. As a result, I always, always, fall back on numbers.

However, I do understand that numbers make some people jittery. Money—no matter how much or how little someone has—can cause stress. In an attempt to try to avoid some of that stress, some of my clients have told me that, prior to meeting me, when times were bad, they never even opened their financial statements!

Fortunately, I love numbers. I devour discussions about numbers, money, technology, stocks, and bonds so much so that I will keep up with all the financial talk radio and TV shows I can—even when my philosophies are not completely in line with the host's. Listening to how the well-known and popular money people advise the public is useful, even though I would never offer blanket advice to any of my clients. My approach to financial advice is that everyone deserves to be treated as an individual. What works best for Mr. and Mrs. Jones does not necessarily work at all for Mr. and Mrs. Smith—and it is not my goal to help the Smiths keep up with the Joneses.

It is my goal to use math and technology to track and measure every decision I make for my clients. This kind of analysis ensures that I am not only providing them with superior service, but am also able to identify where I could or should do better. By running the numbers on the data that is available, I increase the chances of being able to find those underrated and overrated investments. I can show clients how their decisions regarding Social Security and paying down their mortgage function together in terms of the bigger picture, and I can calm clients down even during a global financial crisis.

To be a good financial advisor (or a good investor, for that matter),

```
        TIME

     TRAINING

   TEMPERAMENT
```

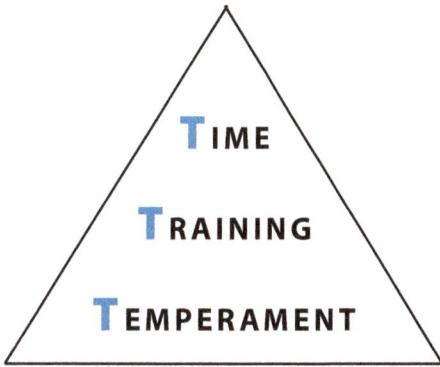

you have to possess three Ts—**time, training, and temperament.** From the moment I sit down in my office chair early in the morning, I spend my workday gathering information for my clients. I'm checking in with Wall Street, I'm reading the latest

> To be a good financial advisor (or a good investor, for that matter), you have to possess three Ts— time, training, and temperament. From he moment I sit down in my office chair early in the morning, I spend my workday gathering information for my clients.

news, and I'm reviewing portfolios using the software I have personally developed. In addition, I am always keeping one eye open for the next Ross Perot or Jack Welch or Warren Buffett.

Training and self-improvement are crucial in my field—and to me, personally—now more than ever. Gone are the days when an advisor could rely solely on what they had learned in the past. Change in this century means that if you have spent the last five minutes staring out the window with your feet on your desk, you have likely missed the birth of some new app, or the rise or fall of one nation's market or another. Taking fiduciary courses at Cal State Fullerton, or refreshing my memory on economic theories, means I can offer better service to my clients.

Providing top-notch financial services also requires a certain temperament. Did my client just read a tweet about the markets plummeting? Is another posting about the next potential "fiscal cliff" trending on Facebook? If so, I know I can expect to hear from some of my clients,

"Ahh! Sell!" When the seasoned financial advisor hears these first signs of panic, he or she often jumps into the phone booth—okay, these days it's the janitor's closet—and changes into a therapist.

"I have done the analysis," the seasoned financial advisor–turned–therapist says to his or her clients. "Rest assured, you own good things and the data is telling us that there is no need to make any hasty decisions right now."

Gradually, clients learn to trust their advisor. When they know their advisor is on top of things and doing his job—and that he defines his job by how well his clients' portfolios, nerves, and lives are faring—they feel better. When their advisor acknowledges their fears, when he sends them weekly updates—as I do—clients will recognize that while Six Sigma accuracy is impossible in the financial realm, a good advisor is maintaining constant vigilance and staying with the math. At a certain point, clients learn when they need to initiate contact and when they can ignore the latest media hype. They know that if the "impending financial disaster" everyone is talking about could affect their portfolio, their advisor is on top of it.

I have read and studied Harry Markowitz's material on modern portfolio theory, which, in a nutshell, aims to guide investors toward the highest possible returns while taking the lowest possible risks.

Eugene Fama and Kenneth French's research into how a company's size and certain other "value factors" have often been an indication of which stocks might do better in the market has also informed the way I research and design my clients' portfolios.

Fama and French started with the observation that two classes of stocks have tended to do better than the market as a whole: (i) small caps and (ii) stocks with a low Price-to-Book ratio (P/B, customarily called value stocks, contrasted with growth stocks). They then added two factors to CAPM to reflect a portfolio's exposure to these two classes:

$$r = R\_f + \beta\_3(K\_m - R\_f) + b\_s \cdot \mathit{SMB} + b\_v \cdot \mathit{HML} + \alpha$$

Source: http://en.wikipedia.org/wiki/Fama%E2%80%93French_three-factor_model

James O'Shaughnessy, a man after my own mathematical heart, devotes hundreds of pages of his book *What Works on Wall Street* to outlining math-based strategies that attempt to explain stock returns. I find myself explaining to new clients time and time again that it isn't so much the "hot" stocks we want to go after, but the undervalued ones—and thanks to O'Shaughnessy, I know how to use the math to find them.

The people I tend to look up to in terms of expertise, experience, and ethics have a few wrinkles—as I do now. More important than the MBA program anyone has just graduated from are those tried and tested three Ts—time, training, and temperament. Those of us with some years under our belts know the true value (and importance) of these key elements.

Some of us remember the days when our parents attended neighborhood mortgage-burning parties—where everyone who had moved onto the same street at around the same time, in the same age and income bracket, gathered together once they had all paid their houses off and literally set fire to their mortgages. Those days were great, but they are gone.

These days, some of my clients' grown children come to me—usually once they have hit their mid forties. They check in to see if they are on the right path. One forty-five-year-old woman came into my office recently and explained to me her plan—she wasn't going to contribute a cent to her retirement fund; she was putting every dollar earned into paying off her house. "Ah!" I said. "But this isn't the good old days." I admired this woman's drive, of course, but the reality of our times is this: If she loses her job tomorrow (which, as we all know, happens far too often these days), how will she take care of herself? When you're hungry, you just can't eat the equity in your home!

"Here's the big picture," I said, and then I went on to explain that, given all we have seen in this young twenty-first century, paying off

> *...if the only tool you have is a hammer, every problem starts to look like a nail.*

your house might make you feel good, but it won't be of much value if you haven't set aside an emergency fund *and* a retirement fund. Period. As much as I understand the desire to experience the feeling of the mortgage-burning party, things are so different today that emulating the strategies that worked in the past may not be the best course of action.

In my early days as a young man entering the world of business, finance, and technology, everyone seemed to know more than I did. Everyone was a genius. I soaked it all up, and I still do. Training as a financial advisor—training for any job—entails more than attendance at a one-time event; it is a never-ending process. I wouldn't be the person I am today, and my business would not be the success it is today, if I had stopped my pursuit of excellence in the sixth grade and become a dreamer of launching lunar modules to the moon. Sure, if I hadn't heard Ross Perot speak (remember his oft-repeated phrase, "Now here's the thing"?), and if I hadn't put double time into all aspects of my adult life, I might be a decent enough financial advisor. But *decent* and *enough* are not words I value, and it is certainly not what my clients— or for that matter, my family and friends—deserve.

Working with my clients is a process I thoroughly enjoy. Striving to be a "genius" in what I do is part of my temperament. In a way, I am the financial world's biggest tool hoarder—if a client needs that special wrench for their portfolio, chances are I have it. And if I don't, I will find it, do the math, and decide if I should use it and store it alongside the rest of my tools. Doing otherwise might mean I'd only have a hammer. And we all know that if the only tool you have is a hammer, every problem starts to look like a nail.

CHAPTER 4

The VanDenburg Technological Edge and What It Means to You (and Your Money)

"The whole is greater than the sum of its parts."
—Aristotle

I expect that many of my readers will remember the old Reese's Peanut Butter Cup TV commercials, where one person carrying a jar of peanut butter would bump into another person carrying a bar of chocolate. Feigned anger would ensue—"You got your peanut butter in my chocolate!" "You got your chocolate in my peanut butter!"—and then each actor would take a taste and realize that the world was a better place when chocolate and peanut butter combined. Mixing two delicious ingredients to make an even tastier product wasn't rocket science, but the commercial was brilliant—it emphasized, albeit in a somewhat silly way, Aristotle's well-known concept that the whole is greater than the sum of its parts.

It isn't surprising that an idea borne of one of the world's most brilliant minds—three hundred and some years before the Common Era—is still completely valid and relevant today. Some might argue that when it comes to technology and the ways in which it can be applied to simplify and improve our lives, Aristotle's claim is truer than ever.

> *When a business utilizes all the data and technology it has at its fingertips, success and growth are practically inevitable. More specifically, when your financial advisor marries math, data, and technology to the fine art of managing your finances—safety, security, and wealth can follow.*

Word, Excel, Access, Outlook, Facebook, Yelp, Twitter—each of these technologies is useful and good on its own. Used in combination, however, they can wield phenomenal power and produce phenomenal results. When a business utilizes all the data and technology it has at its fingertips, success and growth are practically inevitable. More specifically, when your financial advisor marries math, data, and technology to the fine art of managing your finances—safety, security, and wealth can follow.

Learning, understanding, and using technology is necessary to stay alive and successful in this day and age, and this fact will likely never be reversed. The changes in technology occur so fast it often takes society months—if not years—to catch up and stay on top of them. Individuals and businesses must push themselves to constantly learn new things if they want to stay ahead of the curve. And cutting edge now is not simply about riding a trend—it is about being a master at whatever business you run. Yes, most people use technology, but the bigger questions are:

✓ **What technology do they use?**

✓ **How do they use it?**

And most importantly for readers of this book:

✓ **Is the technology your financial advisor uses customized to meet your specific needs?**

As a former software consultant and business optimization specialist, I, of course, use all of the standard office tools and software. I use Word, Excel, Access, and Outlook, for example, where they fit. But when these tools don't do what I want or need them to do, **I will often write custom software so that I am able to accommodate my client's specific and often unique needs.** This does not mean I spend days and hours writing one unique program for each of my clients—that would be wasteful. Rather, when I see a problem that affects a number of clients and can create software that will add value and save time across the board, I make it happen. Furthermore, because I know how to make all these tools work together, I am able to bring to life for my clients the saying "The whole is greater than the sum of its parts."

> *I, of course, use all of the standard office tools and software. I use Word, Excel, Access, and Outlook, for example, where they fit. But when these tools don't do what I want or need them to do, I will often write custom software so that I am able to accommodate my client's specific and often unique needs.*

In order to best serve my clients, I utilize technology in relation to their investments and in relation to their personal needs and desires.

The skills I use to develop custom programs are fairly straightforward, but have been acquired over thirty years of using technology to solve complex problems. I understand what the capabilities of my hardware and software are, and I understand how to design a solution that not only solves the problem at hand but also scales to potentially handle similar situations for others. I have mastered a broad variety of programming languages, and I leverage the most appropriate ones to solve the problems they are best suited to handle. Putting some of the code I have written up here might put many readers to sleep, and would possibly obscure the fact that financial advising is not a mere act of math and science, but also an art—so I'll leave the code in my machine and explain instead how it works its beautiful "magic."

In order to best serve my clients, I utilize technology in relation to their investments and in relation to their personal needs and desires. Every financial advisor learns very early in their career that the first question you ask your client is: What is important about money … to you? (With that ever-crucial emphasis on the pause between *money* and *to you*.) The next step is the first tool in the financial advisor's toolbox, the ever-famous fact-finder sheet, which, as all good advisors know, involves much more than entering the data and letting it sit there.

A good financial advisor takes note of and values things like the client's date of birth, date married, and date employed, but we also take into consideration the facts and data that are subject to change: What does our client need, want, like, and dislike? What kind of retirement experience is he or she hoping for, and how can we use the data about their investments in order to find further opportunities and provide superior service?

One of the most important concepts I explain to my clients is that I am not collecting their information and deep, dark, personal money secrets to mine data in a nefarious NSA way, but in order to always be able to identify opportunities for improvement and to provide superior service to them. Again, my reliance on the Six Sigma approach to measuring everything so that I can identify areas of defect or areas for improvement helps me work smarter and better for each and every client. The programs I run throughout the night alert me the very next morning—and again, I'm in my office by the time the markets open—so that I am ready to address any changes in the world market that might affect any number of my clients.

These programs work together so that I know if a client has become overallocated here or there, or if the income challenges they've been facing for the past six months need addressing or are about to dissipate.

The tools and processes I use and create allow me to swiftly and directly address complex problems, and this kind of efficiency results in superior customer service. My clients know I work with software I have personally tailored to them and their investments—something they know they are not likely to get from any other financial advisor.

> *The tools and processes I use and create allow me to swiftly and directly address complex problems, and this kind of efficiency results in superior customer service.*

That said, the use of technology is not unique to me. However, my personal observation is that many people out there use a tool like Excel as little more than a simple adding machine (or, worse, as a notepad). Sadly, while they are using Excel,

My clients know I work with software I have personally tailored to them and their investments—something they know they are not likely to get from any other financial advisor.

they simply aren't getting everything out of it that they can.

Also, many people don't know how to run database queries to learn things about their clients and their investments. When you have a large number of clients, it pays—trust me—to invest time in learning not only the individual components and advantages of modern technology, but how to use them in tandem.

One of the factors I need to stay on top of in order to understand a client's complete financial situation, for example, is how much their home is worth—that is, how much equity they have. Many financial advisors do this, and many will go to Zillow (a website that will provide an estimated value of a given residence), enter in their client's street address, see what Zillow says, and then enter that information into a spreadsheet to see if the client might be able to refinance, take a reverse mortgage, take their equity and move to a smaller place, etc. This can be a very time-consuming exercise (especially if you have many clients who each have multiple properties), but it needs to be done so that we always have an accurate picture of a client's financial situation.

By writing a small program that goes out to Zillow every night and gets the current values for my clients' properties and reports to me the next morning, I know if there is something I might want to look at. Running my various programs overnight, in tandem, saves me the time I would otherwise spend doing routine tasks by hand during the day (or having to hire lots of staff, which could raise costs), which means I can devote more time to other, more important tasks.

Frankly, I just don't like to waste time and energy on activities that do little or nothing for my clients. I could, like many other advisors, manually hunt for the things that would benefit my clients, but odds are that at the moment I am looking left, the opportunity exists on the right—go ahead, picture your advisor playing the Whac-A-Mole game. Without the appropriate technological tools, such as the types I have purchased or developed, the odds of being able to provide individualized attention and service are reduced, or at the very least, they could be compromised. As you know by now, I don't compromise when it comes to helping my clients.

By combining data about my clients' investments, for example, with the simple Yahoo! tool that allows me to see all the latest news about those investments, I can easily see which investments have something newsworthy about them that I may need to review. With this knowledge, I can easily determine whom I need to call and what actions may need to be taken. If you will, my technology advantage allows me to spend more time *doing* and less time looking for what to do.

Technology allows me to put my arms around each unique portfolio and watch it grow. I am able to manage a large number of portfolios on an individual basis, not by performing some David Copperfield sleight of hand, but because I have been able to put the technological equivalents of chocolate and peanut butter together to create something that is truly spectacular. I take advantage of math, computers, the Internet, and my human touch.

That said, technology is not a magic bullet, and it certainly does not guarantee that everything I want to do will go as smoothly as I would like. The truth is that there is no data available—no matter how mighty our computers become—that tells us what will happen in the future. And there are no computers or programs I could build that offer what I ultimately offer—humanity.

For example, if all I did as a financial advisor was follow the data (which, as we know, is by its nature backward looking), I would believe that now might be a good time to invest in bonds. Data that computers have collected over the past forty years shows that bonds have done very well and have often been considered a safe haven from stock market volatility. However, because current interest rates are at or near historic lows, the reality is that it is very likely that interest rates will rise from here. And when they do rise, the value of bonds is likely to fall (something they really haven't done to any great degree since the mid 1970s). Imagine: you do what you've always done—flee to bonds to get away from stock market volatility right at the moment when interest rates rise. As a result, you actually *lose money* by going to the investment that you perceived as safe.

The reality is that it takes a real live human to know this and to put it all together, and nothing gives me greater satisfaction.

Clients know I never forget a special anniversary or life event. Okay, in some cases perhaps my computer reminds me, but the human in me writes out the card. The human in me is empowered by the technology I have taken the time to learn and take advantage of to provide service neither human nor computer could do alone. In our initial meetings, when the client and I are discussing goals and reviewing forms, I pay close attention so that in the months and years to come, the information I collect never strays from the forefront of how I manage their money and communicate with them. For example, I try to gauge—very early on in our relationship—whether or not sudden moves in the market make a client nervous, so that I know later to give that client a heads-up if I see something I think might concern them. Furthermore, by asking clients whether they prefer a specific level of cash in their account, or how to handle new deposits when they appear—I will know how to best monitor client cash balances and liquidity. I will also know when to reach out and make a call.

Tying all of the intricate components of a client's financial picture together may at first seem challenging. Does it require a huge amount of commitment and time on the financial advisor's part? Yes, but in the end, it is worth it and clients deserve it. Allowing technology to do a portion of the work for me is much more efficient and beneficial to all in the end. To be fair, while I do believe that the appropriate use of technology is a necessity in today's fast-paced world, I must also admit that staying on top of the economy, the markets, investment theory—and yes, technology—also fulfills my personal needs as a lifelong learner. If I'm not involved in a continual process of learning, I might as well call it quits—and that's not likely to happen! My lifelong quest to acquire more skills and to "get more done before nine a.m. then most people accomplish all day" spurs me to get results that I am proud of for my clients.

> *...while I do believe that the appropriate use of technology is a necessity in today's fast-paced world, I must also admit that staying on top of the economy, the markets, investment theory—and yes, technology—also fulfills my personal needs as a lifelong learner.*

I have never been one to follow a pre-defined checklist with my clients, accomplishing a given set of tasks at the first meeting, and another at the next. Financial advising isn't sales to me; it is about service. I understand that earning a client's trust is not a box to be checked off on a data form and then entered into a computer and forgotten. Finances are an emotional trigger for everyone—for those with loads of money and those with more modest amounts—so I don't think there should be any rush to sign on the dotted line.

When a new client comes to me for the first time, we often spend the majority of the meeting talking about what they want to achieve, and the rest of the time reviewing what they've done up to that point to try to achieve those goals. I hold no judgment, and no hidden agenda. I want, as Sergeant Joe Friday often said, "Just the facts." I sell them nothing; I tell them only what I think could be done to help them reach their objectives.

CHAPTER 5

Buy and Hold Isn't Always the Best Plan, for Everyone, Forever

"You got to know when to hold 'em, know when to fold 'em."
—Kenny Rogers

"I purchased that stock back in the '60s and now look at it: today it's worth millions! Are you telling me that what I did wasn't smart?" Financial advisors hear this type of story on a regular basis—someone purchased something a long time ago, and if it did well they tend to believe that *buy and hold* is simply the best way to invest. Their current, potentially commission-based financial advisor might even reinforce that belief. However, we all know that there are very few absolutes in the world, and even fewer in the financial services industry. So is buy and hold really the best plan for everyone, young and old, today?

There are no market absolutes that last forever, and there are no financial-planning panaceas for any one segment of the population, much to the chagrin of the TV financial evangelists. There are only trends and cycles, spikes and dips across sectors, and a series of never-ending unexpected life events for us all. And so, we concede without issue in this chapter that buy and hold can be a good plan, depending on a client's age and other factors. And we say in the same breath that sometimes the time comes when a buy-and-hold strategy should be abandoned.

Investopedia shortly and sweetly defines buy and hold as "A *passive* investment strategy in which an investor buys stocks and holds them a long period of time, regardless of fluctuations in the market. An investor who employs a buy-and-hold strategy actively selects stocks, but once in position, is not concerned with short-term price movements and technical indicators."

The page further explains, "Conventional investing wisdom tells us that with a long time horizon, equities render a higher return than other asset classes such as bonds. There is, however, a debate over whether a buy-and-hold strategy is actually superior to an active investing strategy; both sides have valid arguments. A buy-and-hold strategy has tax benefits, however, because long-term investments tend to be taxed at a lower rate than short-term investments."

In my view, the most critical aspect to take away from this Investopedia material on a buy-and-hold strategy is this: you've got to have *time*.

When drilling for oil, we know that at a certain point, the well will dry up. Oil is a depleting asset—we will run out of it eventually. The same is true about time: the older

> *When drilling for oil, we know that at a certain point, the well will dry up. Oil is a depleting asset—we will run out of it eventually. The same is true about time: the older we get, the more we run out of time. As we age, the long-term aspects of investing need to be evaluated in a completely different light.*

we get, the more we run out of time. **As we age, the long-term aspects of investing need to be evaluated in a completely different light.**

My clients may be holding on to the highest quality blue-chip stock—the kind of salt-of-the-earth stock every American is proud to own, the kind you hold on to for fifty years. But consider this, I tell these clients: holding on to something for fifty years might have made sense when

Buy and hold got many people where they are today, but it may not be the best strategy for getting you where you want to go next. "The times are changing" sounds like a cliché, but it's never been truer.

you were twenty years old, but does it still when you are seventy? Buy and hold got many people where they are today, but it may not be the best strategy for getting you where you want to go next. "The times are changing" sounds like a cliché, but it's never been truer.

The buy-and-hold strategy of yesteryear was built on the premise that you had time, and that time would allow you to weather volatility in the market. But for my clients, many of whom are age sixty-five or older and at or near retirement, the road ahead is not quite so clear. The idea that you can simply hold on to something and eventually it will rise in value starts to make less sense as you begin to lose more of your most precious depleting asset—time. Can you really afford to wait however long it might take for a "bad" investment to recover simply because that strategy has always worked for you? Of course, I'm not saying that "bad" investments do not turn around, but I am saying—as insensitive as it may sound—you might not be around to see it happen.

Retirement is something most people look forward to, but there is no denying it comes with its own pressures, especially now that we are all living longer.

- ✓ **Will we outlive our money?**
- ✓ **What happens if my spouse or I become ill and need home care?**
- ✓ **Can we spend as much of our hard-earned money as we want and still leave some to our heirs?**

Retirement is something most people look forward to, but there is no denying it comes with its own pressures, especially now that we are all living longer. Will we outlive our money? What happens if my spouse or I become ill and need home care? Can we spend as much of our hard-earned money as we want and still leave some to our heirs?

Time, health, and leaving a legacy are major retirement-planning issues, and given the economic roller coaster we all survived in the past five years (not to mention the many others before that), we come to those concerns with much less certainty than we used to about how our money will serve us.

During the major market correction that occurred between November 2007 and March 2009, even the folks who thought that they had more money saved than they would likely ever spend lost out. For example, if you were a devotee of buy and hold and you had $2 million worth of investments in the stock market in November 2007, you likely only had $900,000 by March 2009. Nobody was spared.

To add insult to injury, no matter how much money you had during this time, if you were using your investments to help support your lifestyle in retirement, not only were you experiencing losses due to the market correction, you were also losing money because you were selling things in a down market to pay for living expenses. In effect, you got hit with a double or triple whammy.

People in all income brackets have seen that they can work and save their entire lives to accumulate wealth, only to have factors beyond their control take half of it away in fifteen months. When all the pressures of retirement come to bear and you add to that a 50 percent pullback in the market, emotional pressures can hit like never before. If half your money is gone, the thought of what one year in a long-term care facility might mean is enough to cause panic—and some investors definitely did panic, pulling everything out in 2009 and never returning, or not retiring when they had planned to.

A pullback of 50 percent or more in the market took its toll, and tempers flared. Things have recovered in many ways since our nation's most recent economic crash, but it took roughly five years to recover the losses. In fact, using the S&P 500 index as an example, it was at its high of 1,520 in November 2007. Jumping forward to March 2014, it had grown to approximately 1,850. While that may seem like a pretty big difference (a 21.7 percent absolute gain), the reality is that over that time period its annual return was a meager 3.4 percent! Not really much to write home about, and certainly not the kind of returns that many investors expect (and potentially need) to achieve their financial goals.

Up to this point, I've mostly discussed the fact that I don't believe in buy and hold because it just takes too much time to recover when things go badly. But there is another, equally important consideration to take into account when thinking about buy and hold: in general, buy and hold is outdated, mainly because the market's playing field has changed. Even as recently as the late twentieth century, we weren't nearly as globally connected as we are today. Think about it: if you

> *The sad fact is that the twenty-four-hour news cycle means none of us can afford to remain solely focused on what happens in the United States. The world is moving at a much faster pace, and news that once took days or even weeks to reach US radios and television sets now takes seconds.*

are sixty-five or older, large portions of your lifetime passed without you ever touching a computer, laptop, or cell phone. You learned much of what you needed to know about what was going on in the world from your local TV news or newspaper.

Nowadays, if something happens in Syria, Portugal, or the Ukraine—you name it—we all hear about it in an instant, and quite often the US market reacts. The sad fact is that the twenty-four-hour news cycle means none of us can afford to remain solely focused on what happens in the United States. The world is moving at a much faster pace, and news that once took days or even weeks to reach US radios and television sets now takes seconds. In the old days, when your average investor wanted to know what was happening in the stock market, he or she checked the ticker tape or read the newspaper—which might have been a few hours or days old. These days, with tools such as Yahoo! Finance, everyone can obsessively watch their investments move up and down throughout a twenty-four-hour time period.

The reality is that there are times you want to hold certain investments, and times when you want to let them go. **It's not that buy and hold was never a good strategy,** because it was, and it's not that it won't ever come back—it might. It's just that, in my opinion, having a passive investment strategy in today's dynamic world simply doesn't make sense.

That is not to say that things that appear risky always get hammered. Again, in my view, a more appropriate approach to any kind of investment and any kind of investment strategy is to making a move away from (or toward) something when the data says you should. Although there are no crystal balls, this common-sense approach does help ensure that investors aren't put in a position of having to hold on to something for a very long time in order to recoup potential losses before making a move.

When signals begin to go off, do what you do at a railroad crossing: stop, wait, and listen. If those signals persist, common sense says get off the tracks.

> *The reality is that there are times you want to hold certain investments, and times when you want to let them go. It's not that buy and hold was never a good strategy, because it was, and it's not that it won't ever come back—it might. It's just that, in my opinion, having a passive investment strategy in today's dynamic world simply doesn't make sense.*

How I wish I had this knowledge when I was younger. At the end of the tech/dot-com bubble of the '90s, when I was not yet a financial advisor, I was not nearly as focused on looking to the financial data as I am today. At the time I relied on my personal financial advisor to help me achieve my financial goals. In hindsight—a favorite term for so many of us who took a hit—my financial advisor's view seemed to be that if a little of something was good, a lot must be great. As a result, my portfolio was terribly overallocated in tech stocks.

At no time did my financial advisor ever do the math and say to me, "Todd, it looks like valuations for these stocks don't make much sense, so we should probably do something else." I can hardly blame the guy—after all, almost everyone seemed to think that things would keep going up and up, to the point that Alan Greenspan, former chairman of the Federal Reserve, labeled the phenomenon "irrational exuberance."

"Irrational exuberance" does speak to the emotional aspect of investing. Wherever money is concerned, we can expect emotion will be involved. But at the end of my "staying too long on the tracks" story, my personal portfolio took a major and unnecessary hit because I didn't receive any advice to make a move when the signals said to. You can bet that when I came into financial services years later, I swore to myself that I would never make that mistake again. As they say, fool me once, shame on you; fool me twice, shame on me.

Over the past few years alone, by going to the math and heeding signals, I have been able to alert my clients to several warning signals, and where necessary, to take action. You probably saw some of the same things (the collapse of financial services in 2007/2008, the "oversold" stock market in early 2009, and the sovereign debt issues in the EU in 2012, just to name a few), but did you do anything about it?

> *The fact that the US market is so globally bound now, and can turn and dip and rise and explode in ways it simply did not during the last century, means my notion of time, training, and temperament is probably more useful now than it ever has been.*

To be clear, I am not the type of advisor to pick the "hot" stock, but I do try to make sure that I let go (when the math says to) before they go up in flames. What I focus on is looking for math-based signs of what appears to be clear sailing ahead—or danger of falling rocks—and taking what I believe to be appropriate action.

For example, after 9/11, in hindsight, were airline stocks something that investors should have held on to? I certainly didn't think they were, so I was a big seller at that time. Sometimes signs are strong and clear like that; at other times, events lead to much slower changes that are much harder to predict. The fact is, we all know that the world could turn upside down and back again by the time this book goes to print—and even if it doesn't, it is likely that some of the signals we are seeing today will prove to be incorrect, and the future will be the absolute opposite of what we expect.

The fact that the US market is so globally bound now, and can turn and dip and rise and explode in ways it simply did not during the last century, means my notion of time, training, and temperament is probably more useful now than it ever has been. You have to have the time to do the math, you need to have the training to know how to interpret what the math says, and you have to have the temperament to actually *do* what the math tells you to do.

...wouldn't you rather make a profit and pay a little in taxes than lose money because of an emotional attachment?

If a client is holding on to a stock because he or she places high emotional value on it ("But my great-great-grandfather owned this stock. This is just what my family will always hold on to!") but danger signals are going up all around us, I will not hold my client's hand only to watch them get run down by the oncoming train.

It is okay to have emotions and emotional attachments—I may be a financial advisor who loves his math and his technology, but I'm human. I hold on to my mother's high school yearbook because I know it meant a lot to her and she is gone now. So I tell these clients that I understand emotional attachment, but I'm not going to

I am going to protect my clients' investments, and if that sometimes means protecting my clients from themselves, I will. No financial advisor can guarantee that his or her clients will never lose at all, but at VanDenburg Capital Management, we endeavor to make well-informed decisions, and we pay serious, competent attention to our clients' short- and long-term financial and emotional needs.

let that emotional attachment force me to keep something that, according to the math, may not be worth keeping anymore (or worse, could damage their financial well-being). Said another way, wouldn't you rather make a profit and pay a little in taxes than lose money because of an emotional attachment?

A good financial advisor will not allow you to stay on the tracks just because you always have and a train hasn't run you over yet. "I've never even heard the train," a client might say. Lucky client! The point is, even if a client has been one to buy and hold his or her entire life, they don't have to ride out that hold stage the whole way. When the math says, "Watch out," I am going to repeat the warning and take action. I am going to protect my clients' investments, and if that sometimes means protecting my clients from themselves, I will. No financial advisor can guarantee that his or her clients will never lose at all, but at VanDenburg Capital Management, we endeavor to make well-informed decisions, and we pay serious, competent attention to our clients' short- and long-term financial and emotional needs.

No matter what our age, one thing is certain: tomorrow we will absolutely have less time on this earth than we did yesterday—and we at VanDenburg Capital Management realize there is a certain sense of comfort and stability in sticking to what you know. We understand that feeling because, after all, it is natural to keep doing what has always worked for you in the past. It is our belief, however, that the wisest investment recommendations are based on a client's ever-changing objectives and ability to tolerate risk, as well as on what is happening in changing domestic and global markets. Blanket recommendations that come from experts on the Internet or from popular television personalities can be interesting, educational, and even entertaining, but our question is: Is this expert really talking to *you*? Because we are.

CHAPTER *6*

Why Traditional Estate Planning May Not Be Enough—Introducing Generational Wealth Planning

"A failure to plan is a plan to fail."
—Ben Franklin

A client once said, "Why are we talking about what I'm going to leave my beneficiaries? That's not really a priority for me!" While I completely understood and appreciated the sentiment, the reality is that none of us truly knows exactly when our time on this earth is going to end, so we need to have a good plan for what is going to happen to what we leave behind after we are gone.

Most people have gone through some sort of estate-planning exercise because most people have heard from popular financial advisors in the media that estate planning is a must—if you don't make a plan, your estate (or your beneficiaries) might end up with far less than you think! It's true: whatever money you leave behind will go to someone. And without a solid plan, that someone could be Uncle Sam just as easily, if not *more easily*, than your beneficiaries.

For most of us, the thought of the probate process and a lawyer we have never met going through our papers after we have died—charging exorbitant rates before our beneficiaries even see one cent—is a distressing prospect. Even if you don't have children—even if you don't have more money than you need—whatever you leave will go to someone. Why not make sure it goes where you choose—a person, a charity of your choice, the creation of a scholarship, or a start-up you believe in?

Pondering all this, most people have likely worked with an attorney and have had a trust created. Creating a trust can be a crucial step in financial planning and people are smart to take it, but the creation of a trust is unfortunately where the process often stops. People meet with their attorney and possibly even with their tax specialist, then they get a few tips from their financial advisor—and bam, they fill out some forms, file them, and believe they are set for life (and death). But this is not always the case.

At VanDenburg Capital Management, we help our clients work through all the essential estate-planning steps, establishing a trust, writing up wills, assigning powers of attorney, and so on. Lacking any of those crucial legal documents could result in all sorts of bad things happening—we named just a few in the paragraphs above, and we'll name more of them below. For now, however, we will focus on how we at VanDenburg Capital Management provide our clients with a deeper level of estate planning with what we call generational wealth planning.

> *Like all the wealth planning we do at VanDenburg Capital Management, generational wealth planning—or legacy planning, as some call it—is an ongoing process rather than a singular event.*

Like all the wealth planning we do at VanDenburg Capital Management, generational wealth planning—or legacy planning, as some call it—is an ongoing process rather than a singular event. To be clear, we look to allow for generational wealth only after we know we have taken care of all our client's financial needs. Once we are assured that the client is living the life they want to in retirement, then we start to think about how to ensure that their beneficiaries will receive the greatest possible after-tax benefit. On top of that, we monitor changes in the economy, government policy, and law that could affect our clients and their beneficiaries.

Going back to the DADIE acronym I learned when I studied computer science—Define, Analyze, Design, Implement, and Evaluate—I am constantly evaluating my clients' needs against current economic, regulatory, and political changes. I never do something for a client's portfolio (or generational wealth plan) and just assume it never needs changing or updating. The E in DADIE reminds me that even though I may have done the right thing for one client at a specific time in their life, I must continually evaluate the situation to make sure that we are still on course.

In the previous chapter, we discussed a few of the pressures that come to bear as one reaches retirement age, and the emotions that sometimes surface as these pressures coalesce. Clearly, we don't want any of our clients thinking they should be doing less, having less fun, or going without so that their beneficiaries can inherit a good chunk of money.

Because everyone's individual view of what they want to happen with their money after they are gone can be different, we recognize that the process of generational wealth planning can vary dramatically from client to client, and it depends on a few critical factors:

✓ **How much money do they have? Do they have more money than is covered by their estate-tax deduction (especially since the government frequently changes this number)?**

✓ **Is the client married? Married couples receive a larger combined estate-tax deduction.**

✓ **Whom do they want to receive their unspent wealth once they pass: children, grandchildren, charities, pets?**

✓ **How much "control from the grave" do they want to have? Do they want to give the money outright, or do they want to place restrictions on how and when the money is paid out?**

Again, we cannot stress strongly enough that generational wealth planning is a process, not an event. People place so much faith in legal documents that all too often they believe what is stated on them is set in stone—eternally valid. The most brilliant legal mind might have created these documents, but ultimately, checking off a box does not guarantee you will actually achieve your financial goals. That is why, as a financial advisor, I often send my clients off to seek legal advice—first, because I am not an attorney and do not offer legal advice, and second, because I want my clients to rest assured that the legal documents they have had created will actually achieve their intended financial goals.

It isn't common knowledge, for example, that when leaving your IRA to your two children, simply listing their names as beneficiaries might become problematic if one child predeceases you. If this happens, did you want 100 percent of your IRA to go to your only surviving child or did you want a portion to go to the children of your deceased child? Would it surprise you to learn that in the majority of cases I've seen, the deceased child's children (your grandchildren) get nothing? That's right, *nothing*!

Right about now, most people will say to me, "Well, that cannot possibly happen in my case, because my trust says that my grandchildren will receive whatever my child isn't around to receive." Unfortunately—and not to come across as overly dramatic—the truth is, *the instructions in your trust do not necessarily take precedence over what you wrote on the beneficiary form for your IRA.*

Not to worry, though. There is a relatively simple solution to this problem, known as the *per stirpes* designation. In a nutshell, this designation helps to ensure XYZ. We make sure that all of our clients' IRAs have this solution in place so that the instructions in their trust match the instructions on their IRAs. To my dismay, I rarely see this special designation on the retirement accounts of incoming clients—and as such, it is usually one of the first things I help them to remedy.

Tax law has changed dramatically too, and even though most of my clients meet with their tax professional yearly, I like to remind them that in that tax meeting they are typically looking back to see what they did over the past year. Their main question is usually, "How can I pay less, given what I did last year?" *Looking back, last year*—meetings with a tax specialist tend to be retroactive. On the contrary, meetings with me are proactive—**with generational wealth planning, we are looking to the future;** we are

Looking back, last year—meetings with a tax specialist tend to be retroactive. On the contrary, meetings with me are proactive—with generational wealth planning, we are looking to the future; we are discussing how to do things so that the beneficiaries of your estate will never be stuck facing a reactive situation.

discussing how to do things so that the beneficiaries of your estate will never be stuck facing a reactive situation.

Let's say for simplicity's sake that the estate-tax exemption is $1 million (it is more than that, but we're setting it at this number to make the math easy), and you have an IRA that is worth exactly $500,000 and equity in your home is also exactly $500,000. You also happen to have two children, so the split will be simple and equal, right? You just leave the house to one child and the IRA to the other. *Not exactly*. Even if your estate will owe no estate taxes after you die—because you don't have more than the hypothetical estate tax limit of $1 million—the government considers distributions from an IRA as regular income. So every penny of the IRA you left to one child is taxable as regular income. But your other child inherits the house fully tax free, taking advantage of the capital-gains tax that "goes away," thanks to what is known as a stepped-up basis. Sound fair and equitable?

Taking the IRA issue even one step further, consider the fact that adding IRA income to a beneficiary's income (assuming they are still working), may very well put them in a higher tax bracket. Sure, they are gaining what you have left them, but the burden of paying extra taxes can never be underestimated.

Remember those pressures, those emotions, those stresses we talked about surrounding retirement and generational wealth planning? Why add to your family's burden after you are gone when there are smarter ways to pass your wealth forward?

To be fair, not everything is about addressing challenges. There are also many opportunities that can be taken advantage of. For example, there are many smart ways to take advantage of the tax code. (Note: this is not to say you should wait until the day you retire to take action!) Let's say you earned $75,000 yearly while you were working. How much do you make the day after you retire (excluding pension and Social Security, of course)? Nothing. While you were working, you were likely in a higher tax bracket, so socking money away into a traditional IRA was smart. The day you retire and your income goes away, you are instantly almost certainly in a lower or even the lowest possible tax bracket.

While you are in that lower/lowest tax bracket, it may be a great time to start a regular conversion of some of your IRA into a Roth IRA. After all, you aren't earning an income from a job any longer, so you could be in a very low tax bracket. Why not use that fact to convert IRA money (money that would be 100 percent taxable at regular income-tax rates if you took a large amount out) into a Roth IRA—an account that you or your beneficiaries can take distribution from without paying a penny of tax? Either you can use that converted money tax free during your lifetime, or your heirs can inherit it tax free. In both situations it becomes win-win.

Not having the time or interest to stay abreast of all the changing tax laws and market conditions and legalese is entirely understandable, which is why we fully believe in the power of teamwork when it comes to financial planning for our clients. And our team isn't limited to the people in our office—we are also in frequent

Anyone who knows me knows I do all this work—I stay on top of the news, I run my DADIE analysis, and I master finance and technology—in order to achieve a certain financial goal for each and every client. My clients know that I never act from a one-time, one-size-fits-all transactional motive, and that I am keenly aware that there may be a time and a place for one kind of investment strategy and not another—for one particular client.

contact with our clients' lawyers and tax professionals. By staying on top of tax law, estate-planning law, and investment law, we can reach out promptly when we see something interesting, or of concern.

Anyone who knows me knows I do all this work—I stay on top of the news, I run my DADIE analysis, and I master finance and technology—in order to achieve a certain financial goal for each and every client. **My clients know that I never act from a one-time, one-size-fits-all transactional motive,** and that I am keenly aware that there may be a time and a place for one kind of investment strategy and not another—for one particular client.

One of the most frustrating problems we encounter is when people get the documents they need to plan their estate, and they check the boxes and have the boxes reviewed, but then they simply forget to follow through when any life changes occur, and thus leave their estate subject to vulnerabilities. We have seen it too many times—these people inadvertently render their estate plans nearly worthless. It can be as simple an error as forgetting after refinancing their home to refile all of the necessary new documents to make sure the home is put back into their trust (because during most refinancing processes, the trust company requires that the home be removed from the trust to complete the transaction).

In today's world, the wise person has to ask, "Is what was set up ten years ago going to work today? What about in another ten years?" Ultimately, we all want our plan to work, no matter what happens to Social Security, to pensions, or to some country on the other side of the world that might rise in power and begin to have more influence on US economics than it currently does.

At the risk of making a pseudopolitical statement, most of us can safely assume that the government will go on spending more than it can afford, and will thus continue to look for more sources of revenue. If it can scrape some wealth away from us after we retire or after we pass on, it will. I tell my clients that I base all of my assumptions on a worst-case scenario, which might seem cynical at first. But I believe this pessimism helps me ensure that no matter who is in charge and no matter what our government does or does not do, my plans for my clients will be financially sound. After all, if we don't do everything we can to take care of ourselves, including future generations of our families, who will?

So what do generational wealth planning concepts look like in practice? Well, before the last market collapse, for example, one of my clients came to the realization that he had more money than he was ever going to spend, so we decided to do a little generational wealth planning and take a little more risk than usual with the excess money by investing it fairly aggressively in the stock market. However, instead of just putting that money into the market and hoping for the best, we used a type of investment that had a feature whereby the beneficiaries would be paid the greater of the account value at the time of the client's passing *or* the highest account balance on any contract anniversary. This contract was signed in mid 2006, and for roughly eighteen months, the account value rose with the market, with the value topping out at just over $330,000.

However, as we all know, the markets started to fall dramatically in late 2007. By late 2008, when the client passed away, the account

> *In today's world, the wise person has to ask, "Is what was set up ten years ago going to work today? What about in another ten years?" Ultimately, we all want our plan to work, no matter what happens to Social Security, to pensions, or to some country on the other side of the world that might rise in power and begin to have more influence on US economics than it currently does.*

Money can never replace the loss of a loved one...

balance was just under $200,000. Had the client and I not come up with a firm plan, one that could take hits as hard as the financial collapse of 2008, his beneficiaries would have had to be content with walking away with less than $200,000. However, because of the generational wealth planning strategies we used, I got to tell them that, instead of only receiving the account balance of $200,000, they would be receiving much, much more. **Money can never replace the loss of a loved one,** but in this case we were able to add to the many gifts their father gave them while he was alive (most of which had nothing to do with money) a check for $330,000.

There are no guarantees that this kind of thing can be done for everyone, or that everyone who does this type of thing will achieve the same results, but it does illustrate the potential benefit of having a plan!

Nothing pleases me more than when a client is able to take advantage of some investing strategies while also taking advantage of certain features of some investment products to create a winning situation for the entire family.

We work to help our clients so that they can live the life they want in retirement and then, after they've done everything they ever wanted to do while alive, help others of their choosing (children, grandchildren, relatives, friends, charities, etc.) do the same. Failing to implement sound generational wealth planning concepts doesn't mean that your hard-earned money will disappear once you are gone. It just means that the government might become a major beneficiary of what you leave behind—if that's okay with you!

CHAPTER 7

Why You Can—and Should—
Pay Me Later: Fee-Based Advising

*"Have you seen Webster's definition of 'broker'? It is the
person that you keep giving money to until you eventually
end up ... broker!"*
—Anonymous

"I've always worked with commissioned brokers because I know
that if they want to earn their commission, they have to work
hard to 'earn my business,'" is what someone said to me recently during
an initial consultation in my office. As I see it, they have it a little bit
right and a little bit wrong.

You think nothing of going into a trusted car dealership or big-name
retailer and working with a salesperson who works on commission.
Your new sedan, your new cocktail dress—you know these things are a
one-time transaction, and it doesn't really matter that the person selling
you these goods may not be around the next time you come looking
for a similar product. In the auto and retail industries (and many other
industries), purchasing on commission works perfectly well for both
the seller and the buyer. The fancier the options or the classier the
designer you choose, the more the salesperson typically gets paid on
the front end.

> *I don't find fault with commission-based brokers—after all, they also have bills to pay and families to feed—but I do think the system is fraught with potential conflicts, and that is why when I started out as a financial planner, I started out as fee based. That was over ten years ago, and I have never looked back.*

In the financial services industry, commission-based sales have been around forever too. The commission-based model has worked, both for brokers and for investors, for decades. It is my contention, however, that the fee-based model is a much better fit when it comes to financial planning and investing because the fee-based model allows me to develop an ongoing relationship with my clients—it allows me to better align myself with my clients' daily lives and with changes in the economic climate.

I don't find fault with commission-based brokers—after all, they also have bills to pay and families to feed—but I do think the system is fraught with potential conflicts, and that is why when I started out as a financial planner, I started out as fee based. That was over ten years ago, and I have never looked back.

The system can be tough on new advisors, and that is why many commission-based folks never make it past the two-year mark. But even before they start in the profession, many financial advisors are potentially behind the eight ball because they are likely never made aware there is another option—starting out fee based. Even when they are aware of the option of being a fee-based advisor, they often don't have the life experience, life savings, and life preparation that I had when I first made the decision to enter this field. As a result, the system by default reels many financial advisors in, sets them down one road, and then puts pressure on them to sell—and as we all know, if you work on commission and you can't make the sales, you probably can't pay the rent.

If we take just a brief look at the sorts of problems this system can create, this means that if a client starts out with a commission-based broker and that broker doesn't make it and leaves the industry, the person who comes in to take over their account (assuming they are also commission based) has little incentive to sit and wait for the investments the prior advisor made to run their course.

These new products may be beneficial, of course, but sometimes you've got to wonder. This is not to say your commissioned broker is consciously choosing products that go against your best interest—you trust your broker for good reason—but the point is made to highlight the fact that the commission-based system fosters a state of continual instability for the commissioned advisor, which prompts a continual need to hunt for new clients and to make additional sales.

On the other hand, fee-based brokers such as myself earn our living by charging clients fees for our service. This means that we do not have to spend the majority of our time scrambling to sell more stuff to our existing clients, and we do not have to constantly hustle to find new clientele. Rather, we can focus our time and energy on managing our existing clients' portfolios and looking for ways to provide even better service. Don't get me wrong—we certainly look to grow our businesses (as any good business owner would), but we don't do it at the expense of the time our existing clients deserve and expect us to spend on them.

When I first left the tech field and turned to wealth management, I applied my ever-trusty DADIE

When I first left the tech field and turned to wealth management, I applied my ever-trusty DADIE process to myself: Define, Analyze, Design, Implement, and Evaluate. I asked myself what I would want if I were on the other side of the table—what would I want my financial advisor doing and thinking?

process to myself: Define, Analyze, Design, Implement, and Evaluate. **I asked myself what I would want if I were on the other side of the table—what would I want my financial advisor doing and thinking?** I also thought back to my experiences with my personal financial advisor at the height of the dot-com bubble and asked myself what kinds of things he and I could have done better.

At VanDenburg Capital Management, it is important that the people sitting on the other side of the desk can sense immediately that we are a company committed to creating value and developing lifelong relationships with clients. As part of that commitment, I often give public seminars for retirees, where unfortunately I far too often discover many investors aren't fully aware of what their investments are costing them in fees and commissions. They also may not be fully aware of what options are available to them.

At these seminars—just as during office appointments—I always take it upon myself to explain to people things that have likely never been explained, such as exactly how commission-based advisors are paid, and how I am compensated as a fee-based advisor. Even if people know their advisor earned a commission on the mutual fund he sold them, they probably don't know all of the other ways fees and commissions impact their investments. For example, many people have never heard of, let alone seen, an important document called the Statement of Additional Information. This document exists in addition to the dreaded prospectus, and it outlines all kinds of additional fees people are being charged, but may have never known about—because advisors are not required to give it out.

To be clear, I believe most people don't mind paying for good service. However, to know that they are getting what they have paid for, they need to know all of the different ways they are being charged. Clients cannot escape fees, but they can educate themselves about them so they can make better decisions for themselves and their families.

In general, when it comes to investments, there are two basic fees: one type of fee is intended to compensate the investment company, and the other type of fee is for the advisor.

Various fees come out of every type of investment, and some fees exist no matter how the investment was purchased (that is, whether it was commissioned or fee based)—the

To be clear, I believe most people don't mind paying for good service. ... Clients cannot escape fees, but they can educate themselves about them so they can make better decisions for themselves and their families.

expense ratios associated with mutual funds, for example. For variable annuities, in addition to the commission paid to the broker, there are ongoing fees for things like mortality and expenses and administrative charges. Understanding where fees are coming from and whom they are going to can help you ensure that you aren't paying more than you should as you strive to maintain or grow your portfolio.

As fee-based advisors, we recommend the investments we believe are of the highest quality, and we make sure the costs and fees are appropriate and manageable over time. We control, too, the second type of fee—the fee that pays us. In a nutshell, fee-based advisors are compensated depending on the balances in our clients' accounts—meaning if the client is making money, we are making money; if the value of the client's portfolio goes down (and we all know this happens at times), the advisor makes less. In other words, the fee-based arrangement puts us all in the same boat at the same time, rowing together toward your destination of choice.

When we tell our clients, "What happens in your account means just as much to us as it does to you," we are not just giving lip service.

If we invest our clients' money one day only to turn around and lose it the next, everybody loses. The same type of incentive does not hold completely true for the commission-based advisors.

Again, we are not trying to pit ourselves against brokers—we are simply making clear that a broker gets paid in advance, so there are no built-in incentives for ongoing service. This means that if you decide to leave your broker, or your broker decides to leave the industry, they got paid their commission up front, so they don't really lose much. A fee-based advisor like me is akin to the guy who might come to your house to mow the lawn. While you certainly appreciate the job that they are doing for you, you certainly wouldn't pay them everything in advance of doing the work, and you won't pay me everything in advance either.

> *...you certainly wouldn't pay them everything in advance of doing the work, and you won't pay me everything in advance either.*

When planning for retirement and building our portfolios, we like to believe the people we are working with are looking out for our best interests, but the reality is that commission-based brokers are really only required to do what is *suitable* for the client, instead of doing what is *best*. In the financial services industry, this is known as the suitability standard.

And that one word, *suitable*, is often misunderstood in the context of investing. For example, if you go to the butcher and tell him you are hosting a barbecue for twenty-five people, he will offer you this cut of meat or that one. He will weigh out enough of this cut and that, and you will be able to feed your guests, probably even with leftovers. You asked for meat; your butcher gave it to you. Given what you asked for, he gave you the most suitable recommendation.

He is not, however, a dietitian. A dietitian would review your entire health profile; he would review your lab work—and that of all your guests—and he would then recommend the healthiest possible meal for each and every one of you. That meal might include some meat from the butcher, but it would probably also include some vegetables and a recommendation as to the proper portion size for each guest. The dietitian would be making a recommendation for what is in your best interest, not just what might be suitable.

The problem isn't that people are working with butchers—in most cases, the butcher serves us well—**the problem occurs when people think their financial advisor is a dietitian, when in reality he may be a butcher.** To be clear, we aren't saying that butchers (or brokers) are bad; just that when it comes to your long-term financial health, we think following the ongoing, personally tailored advice of the dietitian is probably a better course of action. That is why, at the very beginning of my career in financial services, I decided to be a fee-based advisor—or, if you will, a dietitian.

> *The problem isn't that people are working with butchers—in most cases, the butcher serves us well—the problem occurs when people think their financial advisor is a dietitian, when in reality he may be a butcher.*

When working with fee-based advisors at VanDenburg Capital Management, clients don't have to worry about the potential inherent conflicts that can exist when an advisor is being paid from commissions, because we are not compensated based on transactions—buying and selling things provides us no additional compensation. We get paid based on the value of our clients' portfolios, so they can be confident that when we buy or sell something that action is based on what we believe to be in the best interest of their account, and not on a need to generate additional income for us.

> *Our clients know we have their financial success in mind above all. Our clients have worked hard to accumulate what they have, and they know that we stay educated in the fields of finance, world markets, and technology in order to help protect those savings. Their money often supports their lifestyle, and we won't jeopardize it.*

Our clients know we have their financial success in mind above all. Our clients have worked hard to accumulate what they have, and they know that we stay educated in the fields of finance, world markets, and technology in order to help protect those savings. Their money often supports their lifestyle, and we won't jeopardize it. The people we work with have often made good choices throughout their lives, and they come to us because they know our focus extends far beyond the current state of this or that particular investment. When the 2008 financial crisis hit, a lot of investors realized for the first time ever the importance of having an advisor by their side who was paying attention, one who was not potentially distracted by the need to chase down more commissions.

People coming to our office for the first time can expect us to run them through a client version of the DADIE process: What is the road you have traveled to get here? Is this road serving you now, or is it time to take a turn? Look at where you were and where you are now: that first car you bought probably isn't as nice as the one you want to buy tomorrow, nor is what you want from your car likely the same today as it was way back when. So it goes to reason that a commission-based model may have worked to get you where you are today because you had the time to ride out the volatility inherent in the markets, and to recover, if you will, from the impacts of high commissions and fees. But do you have as much time to recover from these types of changes and impacts as you did when you purchased your first car—and now that you know there are alternatives, do you want to wait?

People coming to our office for the first time can expect us to run them through a client version of the DADIE process: What is the road you have traveled to get here? Is this road serving you now, or is it time to take a turn?

Our clients are often surprised to find that when they work with us, for the very first time they are working with a team that cares about relationships as well as dollars and cents. When we first meet with clients, they immediately sense that our process is different: rather than being sales driven, it is outcome driven. That is, we at VanDenburg Capital Management are asking what outcome our clients would like to achieve and what investment tools we can present them with in order to give them the best possible chance of achieving those goals.

CHAPTER 8

What's the Next Step?

"A journey of a thousand miles begins with the first step."
—Lao-tzu

I am not trying to take over the world, but I am trying to change the way people interact with their financial advisor. I may have been drawn to the financial services industry partly due to my love of math and problem solving, but it is the human interaction that compels me to get to

> *I am not trying to take over the world, but I am trying to change the way people interact with their financial advisor.*

my office as early as I do every day (again, I am typically sitting at my desk when the markets open at six thirty a.m., Pacific time).

Why, you might ask, do I get to the office so early? One answer is that I want to make sure that I am available. In my opinion, the human element is missing now in too many of our daily tasks—we call the bank or the cable company and we have to push seventeen million buttons before we are allowed to speak to a real live human being.

Sometimes you do the waiting and the button pushing and your call gets dropped. Sometimes you finally do connect, but with whom? This person may be continents away, and you will never talk to him again, even if he tells you his name is Michael and his employee number is 1234. Frustration settles in before you even pick up the phone to make certain calls, and as a result, mistrust grows. Again, though I am not trying to take over or save the world, I am diligently trying to make the call or the visit you make to me—to talk about your money and your future—something you look forward to.

I have always looked forward to learning and improving. If being a student truly were a legitimate career, I would be the poster child for it— most of my clients know I might be enrolled in a few semester-long classes at the local college at any given time. Bettering myself has always been part of my nature. Putting myself on both sides of the desk—as a learner and a teacher— allows me to engage with experts and to provide expertise. And I don't just limit my interests to economics, finance, and technology. When one of my daughters decided to become a triple jumper, I immersed myself in the world of triple jumping. By learning all there was to learn about the hop, skip, and jump, and by engaging other experts, I was able to give my daughter advice, and I could also talk with the coaches on a deeper level than most track fans could.

> *I don't expect all of my clients to become experts on statistics and foreign and domestic economics, but I can certainly help them gain a clearer understanding of why I am investing their money the way I'm investing it.*

Distilling what I have learned in my years as a professional financial consultant and student brings me a deep sense of satisfaction. I

don't expect all of my clients to become experts on statistics and foreign and domestic economics, but I can certainly help them gain a clearer understanding of why I am investing their money the way I'm investing it. Many of my clients tell me that the weekly updates I send out spur them to take a greater interest in economics and the stock market. One goal that I strive to achieve, without a doubt, is to help my clients understand more than they thought they were capable of understanding when it comes to their own money.

We understand that quite often, people have been with their financial advisor for a long time, and the thought of meeting with another advisor has never occurred to them (or has maybe even seemed a little scary).

Managing people's money is very important to me, but people deserve someone who cares about more than just their money. If your mother were sitting across from her financial advisor today, wouldn't you want to know whether her advisor was a butcher or a dietitian? Clients tell me they knew the moment they sat down with me that they were meeting with someone who would work to make things right, if things ever felt wrong. Clients know I am a financial advisor who understands and respects how important their money is to them.

We understand that quite often, people have been with their financial advisor for a long time, and the thought of meeting with another advisor has never occurred to them (or has maybe even seemed a little scary). I always say to these people, "I would never presuppose that your advisor is doing or has done anything wrong. To the contrary, the assumption is that you've been with them for so long because you believe they've been doing right by you. That said, what harm can come from a second opinion?"

> *In fact, we are so confident that a consultation with us will be valuable that we offer a unique satisfaction guarantee.*

Those who decide to meet with me almost always discover there is value in the hour we have spent together and decide that they want to meet again to learn more. However, they are certainly under no obligation to do so. By the end of our meeting, if we find some things that we think could be done better or differently, we let the investor know exactly what we think they should be doing. If they choose, they can take the information we provide them to their existing advisor to implement, or they can work with us. In the end, the choice is theirs (and we never put any pressure on anyone to make any changes).

✓ SATISFACTION GUARANTEE

In fact, we are so confident that a consultation with us will be valuable that we offer a unique satisfaction guarantee.

If someone comes into our office, bringing copies of their investment statements, tax returns, insurance contracts, trusts, etc., and thinks that their time was not well spent, **we will donate $100 to the charity of their choice.** We don't want people to fear getting a second opinion, so our satisfaction guarantee is our way of letting people know that we are serious about trying to find ways to help them achieve their financial goals (whether it is with us or with someone else).

Because we at VanDenburg Capital Management have developed a reputation for being committed to the lifelong education of ourselves and of our clients, we continue to grow. Too often in the financial services industry, businesses begin to seek out wealthier clients as they grow bigger. The logic is that it is better to have 10 clients with $10 million each than 400 clients with $250,000 each. My company is expanding, as I've said, but never will we decide whom we work with based on how much money they have.

> *...we work with people we believe we can help and with whom we want to develop lifelong relationships—period.*

At VanDenburg Capital Management, we work with people we believe we can help and with whom we want to develop lifelong relationships—period. Our clients entrust us with more than their life savings—they entrust us with their lives, and we are incredibly protective of them.

Clients who have been with me for years have watched my business grow from one small room located over the Santa Rosa Chamber of Commerce to the roomier and more accommodating space we reside in today. As we've grown, our clients have never felt a lag in the system along the way, and future clients won't either—because long ago, in the military, I learned the value of being prepared. For example, in anticipation of our next growth spurt, we have hired a new full-time employee and have invested in a new phone system (and other technology) in order to be better able to handle our clients' needs. When our new employee came on, we invited her in as though she were family and asked, "Stepping into our offices for the first time, is there anything you would change?" We never assume that the way we've been doing something is the way it has to be done forever. DADIE just wouldn't allow it!

We at VanDenburg Capital Management are not afraid to ask questions, and we are not afraid to change if change is deemed beneficial to our clients. The bottom line is: we are a family-style business, and though we are continuing to grow, our level of service will never be compromised. With every new client we welcome, we imagine our own mothers sitting in that chair across from us, and we ask how we would like our mothers to be treated here today—and how we would like them to be treated long into the future.

Disclosures

Any tax or estate planning information contained in this book is general in nature. It is provided for informational purposes only, and should not be construed as legal or tax advice. Always consult an attorney or tax professional regarding your specific legal or tax situation.

Different types of investments involve varying degrees of risk, and there can be no assurance that any specific investment will either be suitable or profitable for a client's investment portfolio. Stocks fluctuate, and there is no guarantee of gain regardless of the investment methodology used. Past performance does not guarantee future results.

NOTES_____

NOTES_____

NOTES_____

NOTES_____

NOTES_____

NOTES_____

YOU DESERVE BETTER

"I can't believe that you're calling me back so quickly, Todd. You do know that it's seven thirty p.m., right? You should be with your family!"

Not every phone call or email requires this kind of immediate response, but as Todd VanDenburg, Financial Advisor and author of *You Deserve Better* explains, "My policy is that when a client calls with a serious concern, I try to answer them before they go to sleep that night." This is just one example of Todd's laser like focus on his clients that he has codified into his unique and highly focused set of Guiding Principles:

- **O** *What am I doing to help my clients today?*

- **O** *What am I doing to improve the business so that I can provide my clients with better service today?*

- **O** *What am I doing to improve myself so that I add more value to the business and can do a better job for my clients today?*

When an advisor starts off with three principles that all include the phrase "better serving his clients," you know you are working with someone who genuinely cares. *You Deserve Better* pulls from Todd's years of experience, and shows you his plan for providing top-notch financial services.

Once you learn how amazing your relationship with your financial advisor can be, you will never think about managing your wealth the same way again.

VANDENBURG

CAPITAL MANAGEMENT
707-578-5800

ISBN 978-0-692-29655-4

90000

9 780692 296554